To you with love

To you with love

Terry Rowe

SOUVENIR PRESS

First published in Canada by
Lester & Orpen, Toronto

First British Edition published 1977 by
Souvenir Press Ltd,
43 Great Russell Street, London WC1B 3PA

Reprinted 1993

ISBN 0 285 62271 4

Printed in Great Britain by St Edmundsbury Press Ltd,
Bury St Edmunds, Suffolk and bound by
Hunter & Foulis Ltd, Edinburgh

CONTENTS

Things We Keep/1
Beginnings/2
A Prisoner/5
How Long/6
Open Eyes/7
Journeys/8
Thanks God/12
Walking/13
To You With Love/15
Love Is Giving/18
Happiness/23
Unknowns/24
Love Again/25
Listen/26
The Road to Love/27
Today — Tomorrow/29
A Trip/30
A Song of Love/31
Together We'll See/32
Sharing/33
Waiting on Madison Avenue/34
Losing Time/35

Central Park/38
Lonely Days/43
Anniversary/45
Take What You Need/46
Missing You/48
An Autumn Letter/49
No Room for Sorrow/50
You/51
A Winter Song/52
The Little Things/55
The Memories We Keep/58
Sundays Again/61
Do You Know Me/62
Come Closer/64
Early Morning/65
Morning/67
Any Place/69
Long Distance/70
Any Sunday/72
Paley Park/74
Home Sick/75
Warmth/77
Jealousy/78
Spring/79
I'm Wealthy/80
Music/81
Keep Searching/83
We Change/85
A Definition/88
Friendship/89
Sharing A Dream/92
Apart Together/97
I'm Watching/98
Rooms/99
Carol/100

THINGS WE KEEP

The memory of a love long ago
is like the old grey sweater with
holes that I keep telling myself
I'll throw away,
some day,
not to-day,
I still need it.

BEGINNINGS

I was picking cotton sixteen hours a day
before I was fifteen.
I remember how sore a back can get,
and I can remember how to pray
for some wet weather
for a relaxing change.

Fingers were raw and red
and my back;
almost as black
as my black brother's
baked in the Arkansas sun.

I learned about life in those fields,
I learned about love,
and hate,
about white trash,
and the lash.

I fell in love at the same time,
or thought so,
it didn't last very long.
One evening just before dark
as the clock struck nine
and a lonely loveless hound
interrupted the silence
with a sad howl
love died.

I was walking,
approaching the outside fire
I saw two shapes,
people shapes
but no talking.
As I drew near
the ear splitting din
made by my heart now
experiencing fear
must have alerted them.

3

My love died in a strangers
arms that night
and it is one of the first times
I remember having cried myself
to sleep.

In the morning before the others arose,
I packed my life
and fled
and like yesterday's love
only memories remained.

I've been in love since then;
many times;
all different from today.
So now that I've unpacked
will you stay.
Please.

A PRISONER

I've been a prisoner before,
but never the same as today.
The doors have been slammed
                                and
windows have been jammed,
but there's always been the
possibility of escape.

But when you are a prisoner
of love,
nothing else matters,
you don't even think
of escape.
As a matter of fact
you sort of hope
there is no way out.

5

HOW LONG

Loving you has made me so happy
that I'm walking on cloud fifteen.

> *Loving you is so much fun,*
> *that at night when I dream,*

It's you that makes the stars shine,
and you that wakes the sun each morning

> *in time*
> *to greet the new day.*

Loving you is happiness,

> *here,*

> *and all around.*

Loving you,

> *how long were you waiting*
> *to be found.*

OPEN EYES

I opened my eyes this morning
and saw the future for a change.

Been looking behind far too long.

It was about time I learned
that the past can't be changed.

The future is what really
counts.

If,
you know,
what you,
want.

JOURNEYS

I've walked for miles
over the back roads,
stood for hours on the highways
waiting for a ride to take
me where I didn't know anyone.
Searching for you.

I've ridden the high seas
and left many dinners floating
the waves,
wishing to God I was dead,
but not before
I found you.

I've been frightened in planes,
and slept on wooden benches
of old friendly trains.
Searching for you.

I've been in love, and out of love
more fingers than I can count,
I've wandered to lands you've read about
and walked those back roads once again.
Searching for you.

I've had Pernod at two in the afternoon
and three in the morning
sitting at sidewalk cafes
falling in love with Paris
and its mademoiselles.
Searching for you.

I've shared sausages and bread,
and my bed,
with frauleins from Homburg to Hamburg,
searching.
I remember most of their names
but I'll bet you
just the same that they don't remember mine.
Why should they.
I was searching for you.

In silence I started to shout,
where are you,
and then, when I thought
I'd reached the loveless end,
there you were,
waiting for me.

Looking up and saying hello
as if we'd known each other
for many years,
my search for you and love
had finally become
a dream come true.

God answered those lonely
prayers I used to send his way,
thank God,
for giving me the time
to find you,
today.

THANKS GOD

When I wake up in the morning
I think of you
and thank God.
When I walk the streets alone,
my imagination buying you all
of the pretty things in store windows,
I think of you,
and thank God.
When I see lovers, strolling in the park,
living and loving as only lovers can,
I think of you
and thank God.
When I go home and silently wait
for the sad shadows of nights to
dance their stories across my blank wall
I think of you,
and thank God
for giving me today,
tonight.

WALKING

I used to walk three miles to school
and the same home again.

Through freshly plowed fields
waving hello to groundhogs out for
a breath of spring's perfumed air.

I was looking for you then,
where were you,
you weren't there.

I wanted someone to share
my handful of fresh curd
swiped when the cheesemaker
had his back turned.
You would have enjoyed
the taste of stolen pleasure.

13

You know,
it didn't take much in those days
to make me happy;
it takes more today,
but then I've got more to share today too.
I've been looking all of these years,. .
sorry it took so long to find you.
Take my hand,
let's walk the rest of the road
of life together,
take my hand,
this walk will take forever.

TO YOU WITH LOVE

To give roses
is supposed to mean
a token
of love.

I can't afford those
green house
specials.

Will you settle
for a handful
of dandelions
that'll give you
sticky hands
as you prepare
them
for
display.

When I was
a young boy
I always looked
for the
biggest
and
prettiest
in the field
to give away
to the
someone
I loved.

So,

why should today
be any different.

I have more love now too.

I'll wrap
my love
around this
fresh bouquet
and like
that little boy
of,
so long ago
I'll give you
these flowers
without the rose,

but,

given with love,

and that's worth more
than the most precious
rose,
ever
to
grow.

LOVE IS GIVING

How many times
have you asked
or been asked
to define love;

can you;

think;

what does it
really mean.

Your love
for your children
is one,
another,
for their mom.

Good music
may be one too,
and you,
you love
as well.

Baseball.

Hockey.

Ice Cream.

Peanut Butter.

19

Can you
tell the
difference.

The word itself
is too often used,
most times the true
meaning
violently abused.

If I say I Love You,
I want it to mean
more than being amused,
by a funny movie,
or,
play,
and, I want it to mean
the same as yesterday.

20

If tomorrow comes,
another day,
but,
the meaning
in I love you
the same
as today.

It could be just living,
but it's not owning,
it could be forgiving,
not being selfish.

But in the end,
to me at least,
it means;

giving.

That's living,
that's loving,

just giving,

not expecting
anything in return,
and as you grow older,

you'll learn,

loving,
is
giving.

Nothing.

More.

HAPPINESS

Can't you understand
that your happiness
means more to me
than my own.

That's what love
is all about,
that's when you know.
When someone else's
feelings mean
more to you
than your own,

it's love,

you'll know.

UNKNOWNS

Have you ever entered a blind alley
frightened
of what's waiting at the other end.
That's what I feel
loving you.
The thrill of the waiting unknown
has grown
inside of me
forcing me on.
I hope there's an opening
at the other end
that we can squeeze through
without hurting each other
in passing.

LOVE AGAIN

It wasn't too long ago we shared
and dared
to learn each other.
I didn't think that I would ever
love again.
That was before I discovered you
and the love I felt in your arms
repaired
the wounds of loves past.

So if I'm quiet, and sometimes
not too gentle,
remember,
this love is as new to me
as it is to you.
I'm trying to remember where I went
wrong so long ago,
so that now I've found you at last
with each passing day our love will grow.

Be patient and understand,
I'll need your hand,
sometimes to lead the way,
be gentle,
so that today will be repeated
day after day.

LISTEN

I want to say I love you,
Yet, I'm afraid that if I do,
you'll laugh, and call me silly.
Because you know what that word
means to me,
and you.
Or maybe I'm afraid that you'll
be afraid too,
and that you'll end this romance
before it begins.
But love can't be stored away,
it's too important to keep within.
So if I say I Love You,
today,
please be gentle, listen,
because I'll be saying it again and again,
without thinking,
without asking for your permission.

THE ROAD TO LOVE

This journey into love is
almost like a trip into the
unknown.
Almost, because I have the feeling
that somehow I've been over this road
before although the last time I made
the trip alone.
I remember some of the rough terrain
I remember the pot-holes
wild branches
and slippery rocks moistened
with tears.
So this time I walk carefully
watching my every step,
I'll take your hand and lead you
guide you,
but you must give me
trust,
and be ready to help me if I slip
or fall if suddenly I'm not able
to see.

If you are not strong enough
please tell me now,
don't wait until we are half way across
when I need you and find
that once again I'm walking alone.
So if you are ready,
take my hand,
and let's slowly, together
walk all the way,
we'll take our time,
pause for breath,
never run,
but love and discover love
with each new day.

TODAY

If I give you
all
of me
today,

If I give
you happiness
today,

If I
love you today,

If you love
me
today,

TOMORROW

what
will
you expect
tomorrow.

will you
give
me sorrow.

I'll give
the same tomorrow

We won't need
to think about
tomorrows.

29

A TRIP

I'm going to take you around
the world and back,
come,
take my hand,
we'll walk around the block.
We'll buy sausages at Schneider's,
cheese from Monsieur Dupres,
some hot green peppers will tempt
you at Luigis,
canned octopus from Jose.
Herring from the Dane
whose name
no one can pronounce.
We'll stop for a glass of wine
and some music at Zorba's,
and finish our tour with dinner
at the Ports of Call.
Come, we are going around
the world,
and when we come back
we'll make love
to the sound of the sea
in stereo.

A SONG OF LOVE

I wanted to write you
a love song.

To give you a souvenir
of my love for you.

Everytime I tried
the words just
seemed to disappear.

They went hiding
in another place.

But words
couldn't really
tell anyway,
and I guess no one
really wants
a substitute
souvenir
for today's
love.

So this is my
love song,
written
just
for   YOU.

The only
words
that
found
their
way
back.

                        I

            LOVE

            YOU.

TOGETHER WE'LL SEE

*I have so many
places to see,
pretty villages
sleeping by the sea,
but it's no fun
to go there alone,
the air wouldn't smell
the same,
the wine would have a bitter taste
and cheese and bread
wouldn't seem to go together;
the bed
would still be cold
even with the three pound
ton of feather,
because there is nothing as
warm as a naked body beside you,
radiating warmth, and perfuming
the room with odours of last night's
love lingering long after night
has fled,
leaving morning stars scattered behind.
We have so many places to see,
you and me,
together.*

SHARING

There's so much I want to share with you,
spring's gentle rain,
ruining today's dry cleaning, and
broken egg yolks and unbuttered toast
in the morning at three in the afternoon.
I want to share all there is left
for us to see,
I want to share so that we,
will become and remain we,
instead of just you,
or me.

WAITING ON MADISON AVE.

I've travelled a million miles
to be with you today.
It's been almost that many,
counting all the years I've been
wandering, looking around.
I've come a long ways
and now,
sitting here in a bar on
Madison Avenue,
waiting,
for the thrill of seeing you
again conjures dreams,
waiting to become real.
An hour from now,
when at last I'll steal
some of your precious time
and never give it back
only because I can't,
and really don't
want to anyway.

LOSING TIME

I wandered the streets all day
waiting for you,
didn't need a haircut
but a few minutes in
a stylist's chair,
(they don't call themselves
barbers any more)
helped waste a few minutes
while I waited for you.
Don't much like drinking
in the afternoon either,
but somehow my feet guided
me into a bar just around
the corner where I shared empty hours
with an empty room,
and watched the hand on a clock
take an hour to move
a minute or two.

Then it was time,
time to arrive
a few minutes late,
and time to begin
where we left off
so many weeks ago
in another place.
And you know it's
never to late
to begin again, because
the thrill of seeing you
gripped me almost like pain.

We've come a long way
you and I,
and as time goes
so will you and I.
And as futures are dreamt
and pasts shoved to the hidden
vaults of our minds,
just being together,
for as many minutes, hours,
days or years
as we can capture
with each other
is all we'll need
to be,
as long as we,
are we.

CENTRAL PARK

Central Park in the afternoon,
safe at this time of day,
probably safe after dark too
although that's not what the
newspapers say.

But, I remember the sunshine
and blue sky,
and tired legs on a bike
that had to be back before night.
Many kinds of people;
some large, some small,
but all
there for the same reason,
to escape
the plastic jungle outside on
the streets.

The air is filled with songs,
and amateur guitars,
steel drums beating life's beat,
the clown entertaining children
with his stories and bells,
his multi-coloured costume
blending with Alice in Wonderland
and her friends,
what stories they could tell.

Sailboats racing over the pond
and grown men chasing them
reliving their childhood
for a few hours;
and dogs, leading their masters
and mistresses
for a Saturday afternoon stroll
some running loose the way nature meant.
Some swimming and chasing sticks
thrown half way across
a pond of imaginary blue
and you,
and I,
sunning ourselves in the sun
on heated stones,
and we were afraid to sleep
to leave the bikes alone
for someone to steal,
the truth in our minds
ever present,
making life real.

But most of all I remember
the togetherness we had,
the looks,
the caresses,
the kisses,
and you
so glad that I was happy
for these few hours.
Your beautiful eyes
filled with momentary love,
life, and hope,
and the pressure of your
hands gentle in their touch
sent warm chills racing
over my back.

And later your searching
lips sent secret messages
to my brain,
and you didn't know
that they were so gently erasing
yesterday's pain.
It was a great day,
today,
easy to recall,
thinking, remembering, hoping,
that's not all.

LONELY DAYS

There are days when I've been alone
but I wasn't lonely.

There is a difference
you see.

Being alone
is because that's
what you want.

Being lonely
is being alone
and not wanting to be.

                    Like me,
I'm lonely.

I know I don't have to be
I'm sure that if I looked
I'd find
someone willing
to share these empty hours.

But I won't,
it wouldn't be fair.

I've given you all
that I have to give,
there's nothing left over
to share with someone else
but conversation,
and most times
that's just
not enough.

I'm still lonely
but because of you
I'm no longer alone.

44

ANNIVERSARY

*I can't remember birthdays,
and anniversaries
don't mean a thing normally.*

Today is our anniversary.

*A blind date,
and I arrived so late that
you wondered if indeed I'd arrive.*

I did.

We started the rest of our lives.

45

TAKE WHAT YOU NEED

I've stopped asking
when can I see you again.
Each time I asked and received
no answer
I saw some inner pain
mask your eyes
and felt that same inner pain
clutch my heart.

I don't want to hurt
and I'm weary of
being hurt
and because I love you
so,
when you leave this time
I know
you'll go
with a little more
of my heart than you
had before.

I've given all
but you only take
as much as you have
room for right now,
no more.

I know and I think
I understand.

Take what you need
for right now,
the rest is waiting
in my open hands.

MISSING YOU

As the blue sky above
would miss the sun,
and if the moon at night
saw no one,
that's how I miss you.
If robins had blue breasts
instead of red,
and if blue jays were red,
instead,
if the ocean had no bottom,
and life no hope,
if love was just a word,
instead of love, the hope,
if dogs had no barks,
and cats no meows,
if children weren't so pure
and had no children's fun,
if all of these were, as it were,
and if you weren't you
and I wasn't sure,
that's what it's like
being away from you,
that's what it is
missing you.

AN AUTUMN LETTER

I wrote you a letter today,
read it over once and
decided to throw it away.
To let the thoughts written on paper
blow away like the autumn leaves
in an autumn wind,
that grows colder each passing day.
Absence makes the heart grow fonder
a wise man said one unthinking day,
I'm not wise, and often have unthinking days
but I know absence has nothing to do
with the heart growing fonder,
it's really memories, and imagination
that keeps me interested.

NO ROOM FOR SORROW

My heart is screaming
please don't go away,
but,
my heart is also keeping these
words within.
I know that if you want
to leave you will,
and if you want to stay
another day
I won't have to ask
and neither will you.
So forget about yesterday,
don't wonder about tomorrow,
love and live today,
it's all the life we've got,
let's not spoil it with sorrow.

YOU

You touched me last night
and awakened the insides of my mind.
Your words
written on paper
gently engulfed me,
my kind.

I waited so long to hear from you
yet I don't know what I expected
to hear.

I guess, I was just hoping
somehow,
to have you near,
to have you close,
to me.

A WINTER SONG

It's winter again,
white snow, cold winds,
fires in fireplaces
aglow.
It's the time of red noses,
and sliding feet,
of hot rums
and other winter treats.
Skis and sleighs
and horses with bells,
frost in the air
and frozen wells.
It's winter again.

It's memories of something old,
something new,
yesterdays', todays',
tomorrows' not yet new.
I didn't use to mind
these winter months
even when I was alone,
but lately, I've come to wish
for spring,
when I hope you'll have some time
to spend with me,
alone,
sipping wine.

It's winter again,
but I understand
your love for the slopes,
the aloneness of skiing,
the joy you feel,
the hopes,
the thrill of breaking virgin
trails in the snow,
the Aprés parties,
the fires,
the warm glows.
I do understand the happiness
you feel,
standing there alone,
on a hill,
the wind gently blowing,
the expected,
unexpected
thrill, waiting below.
The excitement,
the roar,
as you swiftly soar
by winter's sleeping trees.

Yes, I understand
even though I'm not a skier,
strange though it may seem
I do understand,
next winter, maybe,
I dream.

So have fun,
do what you enjoy,
take all of the pleasure
you can get,
for this way I'll be
giving,
and later,
when winter is over
it'll be your turn to
give,
and mine to forget
these long winter nights
and the loneliness you know I feel.

Have fun,
I understand,
it's your winter,
I'll be waiting,
near the sand.

THE LITTLE THINGS

It's the little
things I remember most,
the left turn attempted on a
red light,
the cool air at night
as we ventured outside.
The way you like your
coffee in the morning
and the softness of your naked
back.
The subway rides so new to you.
The silences we enjoyed together,
the music that seemed to go on
forever.

I remember the lost keys,
and the sun above,
and please,
or thank you.
The unbitten, broken finger nail,
the trails
of scented smoke
wending their way around
our heads
and the silent beckoning of the
warm bed
on a warm afternoon.

I remember these little things
that don't seem worth much thought,
but to me these kind of memories
are worth a lot.
So,
I'll keep them,
recall them
when I feel a little low,
think about
not seeing you,
and maybe for a time,
these thoughts
and memories
will help
to keep that warm
feeling
inside
aglow.

THE MEMORIES WE KEEP

I've been alone so long now
that I'd forgotten there
could be someone who cared
enough to
hope that I'd call.
Man is that way,
he must be told,
why.
I guess it's because he's afraid
that what he wants to be true isn't
and he doesn't want to find out.

You know it's much safer sometimes
to live with hopes
and past memories
rather than see the truth
about tomorrow,
because you never learn
how not to be hurt,
and the pain,
sometimes is too high a price
to pay when you are not sure.

I guess that's why
we try
to borrow more time,
we try
to share with memories
the happiness
that was there,
once upon a time.

SUNDAYS AGAIN

Sundays won't ever be
the same again
without you.
Come to think of it
Mondays to Saturdays
are going to be
different too.
The days and nights
will still come and go,
the sun will sometimes shine,
and the stars will sometimes glow,
and as we travel
from week to week,
walking and running,
our brains being guided
by our feet,
the thoughts and memories
will be all that's needed,
to remind us that for once,
our hearts,
we heeded.

DO YOU KNOW ME

Don't let your imagination fool you,
I'm not really as nice as I seem.
I have many faults
and really am only that nice
in your dreams.
The difference is that I know,
so I'll be careful,
careful, not to hurt.
I know and I'll try
never to make you cry;
not from sadness anyway.

But when you love
if you really do,
it's impossible not to
expect some pain.
For when you really love,
the pain
sometimes is worth the
chance to learn
about this love,
and loving,
not making the same
unloving mistakes
once again.

COME CLOSER

Does my wanting you near
frighten you.
I hope not.
I can't hide
these tender feelings
no matter how hard
I tell myself I'm trying.

I've told myself to be careful,
not to rush you
with my thoughts;
but we have so much left
yet to share
that in my hurry
I'd rather think of the
haves,
and forget for once the
have nots.

EARLY MORNING

I said good-bye when
I left this morning.
You didn't hear,
although,
you seemed to gently
smile
as I whispered a kiss
tickling your ear.

Last night's love
was more than I
could take so early
in the morning
within the confines
of this loving in room,
I had to leave,
walk in the park
breathe spring's air
and let the symphony of the meadowlark
provide the background
music for my love thoughts.

Don't worry, I'll be back,
I'll return before you awaken.
I'm bringing you a loaf
of freshly baked bread;
that was my other reason for leaving
or so I told myself.
What I really wanted to do was
to show off,
to shout my love for all of the
outside world to hear.
You must have been listening
because now that you are wide
awake
I can see the naked love in your eyes,
and once again I'm reminded
that even when I'm outside
alone,
you are near.

MORNING

I remember how I used to lay beside you
awake at dawn,
pretending to be asleep,
hoping you would awaken
and get up,
put the morning coffee on.
But then you would stir
and the soft fur
on your body was electric as
it caressed my back.

I remember how the nipples of your
firm breasts like nuggets
imprinted themselves as you snuggled
closer.

I smiled as love murmers escaped from
your throat like a gentle breeze
tickling.
All enough to help me change my mind,
and encourage me to steal out of bed
to make that coffee for both of us.

Then when it was ready
I'd try to sneak back with
steaming cups to find you
awake and smiling.
The laughter in your eyes told me
you hadn't been asleep either.
I'd put the cups down, leap at you
to tease you for testing my love;
later;
much later;
we'd sip coffee now ice cold
and I would dream
of growing old,
with you,
each of us together,
each of us loving,
forever.

ANY PLACE

I wish my hands could reach across
the miles of space
that separate us,
just to touch your face.

> *And, I wish my eyes could see*
> *as far*
> *as I would need,*
> *to read*
> *your eyes,*
> *to once again see*
> *your beauty*
> *already engraved on my mind.*

> *I guess it really doesn't matter*
> *because my heart;*
> *though small it might*
> *appear to be,*
> *is big enough,*
> > *is strong enough,*
> > *to reach out,*
> > *and touch,*

to shorten any distance,

wherever   you   might   be.

LONG DISTANCE

It's hell not being able
to see you,
and it's disappointing to call
and not hear
your voice at the other
end.

Another whole weekend
without you.
But,
I'm still alive on the outside
and it's those secret hopes
that keep me
alive,

inside.

ANY SUNDAY

It's Sunday morning again,
it arrives every week at the
same time.
The radio beside my bed that has
been playing music all night
now takes a break and is
bringing us up-to-date,
News:
nineteen people killed on the highway
this week-end,
a record of another kind,
and as I bend
to start that first cigarette of the day
I think of Sundays past,
and those other days in between,
left over memories,
sometimes found in dreams.

I still make coffee the same way,
a dash of salt, hot and black,
but it doesn't taste the same
without the comfort of your back
resting against my belly.
The silence of the aloneness all around
makes me shiver from the cold
of being alone,
and the emptiness I feel within me,
makes me afraid,
afraid once again
of growing old,
alone,
and I close my eyes
and think of your love;
and today's Sunday pain,
once again
is erased,
until next week at the same time.

PALEY PARK

You know waterfalls
seem so friendly,
I guess it's because
they are full of life,
but who would have believed
that one would have found,
such beauty, peace, and so much love,
here, downtown.

We found it,
and much, much more,
perhaps that which we were
searching for.
The chilly wind brought us
closer together,
and hot coffee forced us to stay
as if we needed that.
Here we found each other again,
just before dark,
here, we fell in love and loved
at Paley Park.

HOME SICK

I hate saying good-bye
and scenes that make
some cry.
I don't like leaving
seems I'm running away,
when really I'd rather stay
looking forward
to tomorrow's sun
and another day
to spend in the safeness
of your arms
where I can gather strength.
Safe in your arms
where it feels like home,
and
I'm needed.

Everyone knows
that running away from home
might be the right
thing to do
at that time
knowing,
that one day you'll return
with less time
left,
such a waste,
such a shame,
such a world,
such a game
we force each other to play.

WARMTH

I like the way your smile
lights up my room.

Your eyes tell me
some nice things too.

It's nice to have someone
to hold once again.

To do little things for,
like covering cold feet
with a spare pillow.

I like the way your warmth
radiates,
heating my room.

My Heart.

JEALOUSY

There are times
when I wish I
could read your mind.
But then again there
are other moments
when I'm glad
that I can't;
especially those times
when I know you are sad.
I guess I'm just jealous
of your thoughts and memories
that don't include me.

SPRING

It's raining today;
feels like I should
be in bed with a good book,
soft music
and you.

I might even read aloud,
so that you could close
your eyes,
and dream away the hours.

It's raining today;
I'm loving you.

I'M WEALTHY

Wealth shouldn't be measured by
the amount of money you have,
or don't have,
but by how many people are your
friends,
and to how many people
you are a friend.
Wealth is how much love
you have to give,
and loving someone
is part of the today fortune
of being able to give.
I love you,
and am very rich indeed,
I love you,
so there's nothing else
in life I need.

MUSIC

Sure I like listening to the
Beatles
and
Peter Paul and Mary.
I dig Grand Funk sometimes
as well as a five string banjo
strummed to the tunes
remembered from yesterday.

But,
when I'm with you and
most other times too,
I'd just as soon listen to
Frank Sinatra
telling us about love
and what it's all about.

KEEP SEARCHING

Don't you see there is no
easy way out for people
like you and I.
Sure, others, some time
friends
will try to drown our thoughts
with their shouts:
what are you looking for,
be happy with what you have,
they don't understand
they don't know that
happiness has no end.

They don't know
that what makes us happy
today
may not be enough for tomorrow,
and yesterdays
for us,
may have been filled
with sorrow.

But we know what we want today
and we can prepare
if tomorrow becomes today,
and in our own way
we continue to search
for the most happiness
we can find,
they don't know
that only this way
can we ever be happy
in our own minds
and that's where it means
the most anyway,
today
or any day.

WE CHANGE

Each one of us change
day by day,
what I think today
is different from what
I might have thought
yesterday.
Last year's thoughts of life
were right for me
at that time.
The thoughts I have tonight
are what's right
for me
today.

Sure we remember what
happened in the past
but we can't live on
those memories
life goes by
those days are past.

It's not what happened
that's really important
in life,
and we can't do anything
about what might come
tomorrow,
if indeed it does,
except wait for whatever,
whenever.

So if all of this is true
and I believe it is,
then what we'd better do,
is live.
Take the most out of what
is today,
and promise ourselves
that if tomorrow comes
we'll be ready for another
day.

We will be prepared to live
and play as well as we can,
without hurting
but loving,
our fellow man.
And it doesn't really matter
who he might happen to be,
cause if we love him,
just think,
we'll all be happier,
him, and you and me.

A DEFINITION

Sadness is happiness
in disguise.

Look within and
you'll see
with your mind's eye
that,
that,
which makes you sad,
is also,
that,
which at one time
made you so very
glad.

FRIENDSHIP

It's not strange that you don't know me,
I hardly know myself sometimes,
I have done things, that later I'd
wished I hadn't
yet couldn't stop from doing again.

> It seems I'm someone today when I'm happy,
> a different person than yesterday
> when I was sad.

Tomorrow I'll probably be
someone else again,
never the same,
but now I won't hurt
or try to cause pain.

It used to bother me what others thought,
but lately I've come to realize
that others too are different.

They might love me today,
hate me tomorrow;
life:
what a plot,
until you realize
what you're not.

I used to complain
that I had no friends,
and then I stopped for a moment to think,
what have I given to make me worthy.

I discovered
and I hope you will too,
that it takes more than being
able to pretend
that you are interested or want to help.

> *It means being and*
> *doing,*
> *without being asked,*
> *most times without even*
> *thinking.*

> *My friends it's not a question*
> *of being able to lend,*
> *it's GIVING,*
> *being a friend.*

SHARING A DREAM

I had a dream last night
one that I shared with you
so many miles away.
We were alone,
just you and I,
a frisky mongrel
looking for love,
we three
and the sea.

The shelves were laden with
winter's provisions,
the wood shed full
and our heads clear
with no time and no need
to make decisions.

We spent our days working,
me with pencil and paper,
you at a piano for a while
and then later I'd smile
as you exchanged the wooden
bench
for brushes and paint.

Time flew by during the afternoons
and we touched each other
with our love.

Once in a while
a tender kiss,
sometimes just
a little more.

We'd spend our days working,
eating when we were hungry
not when told to by
a clock or the sun's shadow
dimming the shore.

Just before dusk
we'd go for a walk
feet sinking in the cool
evening sand and
gently bruising toes
as we kicked white pebbles
with our bare feet.

And we'd stop every
once in a while
to wet our hands in the
friendly sea.

Beauty,
God's beauty unfolded
before our eyes,
the red ball, today's sun,
blinking to us
today's good-bye.

And on we'd go,
holding each other,
and rough warm woolly sweaters
and love
keeping in the warm.

We'd walk and walk
neither one of us
bothering to talk,
there was no need,
because we loved
we were as one,
and no one to heed.

Then I woke up
and as I tried to
reach across the miles
of space that separate us
I discovered reality
and the fact that
you weren't there.

We haven't been for that
walk by the sea,
and those imagined footprints
in the sand being filled so
rapidly was really a beckoning signal.

Telling you,
telling me,
look,
this is what could be.

APART TOGETHER

I can't be your mind
nor do I want you to be mine.
In loving each other
we must stand apart
and yet be one,
using understanding
as the force that will
keep us separated,
and yet,
forever together.

I'M WATCHING

You can't fool
small children
and animals,
some say.

It's true
because that's
why,
without motive,
with children and animals
we,
for once,
are our true selves.

I hope I don't ever see
a dog bite you,
or a child,
afraid to look
you in the eye.

ROOMS

Bar-rooms,
men's rooms,
bed rooms,
living rooms,
dining rooms,
pool rooms,
school rooms,
motel rooms,
hotel rooms,
waiting rooms,
state rooms,
board rooms,
whore's rooms,
I've seen them all,
lived in them too
at one time or another.

If you were to ask
which did you prefer
I'd have to ask when.
Because at that time
I liked that room,
then . . .

CAROL

You are so new to me
this love is like spring's
buds on trees,
each day growing
soon to blossom and become
summer's leaves.

When summer passes
Fall will come and
its passion
will kiss the leaves
and mature the colours
preparing
them for their resting
place
as winter's gentle blanket,
helping to keep in the
earth's gentle warmth.
So will my love grow
and mature,
my love will keep
on living
of this I am sure.

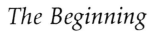

The Beginning

Terry Rowe was born in Peterborough in 1936, and grew up in the farm country of Ontario. Since leaving home at the age of 13 he has travelled throughout Canada, the U.S.A. and Western Europe. He has worked as a shoe shine boy, laborer, short order cook, circus clown, carnival barker — he has picked cotton, strawberries and sold insurance. He has spent some years in the Royal Canadian Air Force as an Intelligence Specialist, has sold Real Estate and has been a very successful public speaker and sales consultant. "To you with love" is his first published collection of love poetry. These prose/poems enter our very private worlds of fantasy, desire, loneliness and survival.

Terry Rowe now lives in Toronto, where he is preparing for a concert tour which will bring him into the major concert halls of North America. His unique style is now available on his first album "To you with love" and includes selected love poems accompanied by original music. Terry Rowe's refreshing style is indeed a welcome change in today's modern and sometimes confused environment. His poems glorify love in all its precious moments through all its seasons. They will be remembered and cherished—a jewel of a gift for lovers everywhere.